A Collection

of

Heartfelt Poems

"Linda Fay" Lynda Minor-Milner

Order this book online at www.trafford.com
or email orders@trafford.com

Most Trafford titles are also available at major online book retailers.

Printed in the United States of America.

ISBN: 978-1-4907-0685-6 (sc)
ISBN: 978-1-4907-0686-3 (e)

Trafford rev. 06/12/2014

 www.trafford.com

North America & international
toll-free: 1 888 232 4444 (USA & Canada)
fax: 812 355 4082

CONTENTS

ACKNOWLEDGEMENTS

First, giving honor to God for His grace and mercy towards me. For without His timely intervention, this wonderful feat could not have been accomplished. Thank you God!!☺

Love,

Lynda

I acknowledge my granddaughter, Gabrielle Gardner, because it was my poem about her called an "Amazing Miracle" that launched this collection.

I also acknowledge the encouragement and support of family and friends, my gratitude and love extend beyond infinity!! Thanks so much!!

My family:

My daughter, Ronetta Milner—Gardner; granddaughter; Gabrielle J. Gardner; neice, Tonia Minor—Benniefield; cousins; Mary Reynolds and Brenda Joyce Richardson.

My friends and associates include: Theta Frasier; Janie Bruen; Janice Maynor; Betty Keitt; Joseph Manker; Janie Powell; Nateriel Powell; Evelyn Smart; Ruby Rawlison; Eldora Thomas; Trustees Ministry of Bethlehem Missionary Baptist Church, and the late, Bettye Ann Battiste

colleagues include . . . .

Vernice Barnes; Irina Gorb; Hollis Peck; Mary Knight (Savannah High School) . . . Zykiah Watts; Dell Willis (Derenne Middle School)

Technical support: Ronetta M. Gardner; Gabrielle Gardner; Vernice Barnes; Hollis Peck and Savannah High School's Media center

~This first publication is dedicated to the memory of~

> My mother, Gladys Porter Minor
> My father, Elijah Minor
> My grandmother, Sweetie Minor
> My grandfather, Cornelius Minor

For the traits they passed to me, and for their love for me!

Also

> To My mother's parents that left her on the doorsteps of a friend in Florida . . . . for if nothing else . . . their traits, too.

And

To my favorite aunt, Rosa M. Thomas who encouraged me through the years in all of my endeavors!!

AN AMAZING MIRACLE

God made me just who I am . . . .
An amazing miracle says my mom and Gram.
Statistics suggested that I should not be here . . .
But God said she shall and will . . . and He made it very
    clear!!
The evidence lies in the beautiful scar,
Revealed everyday in my life thus far.
I've never hidden it,
Nor ever been ashamed of it.
For it is a constant reminder of God's love . . . .
As he talks to me everyday from above.

Gabby, He says you are here for a reason,
To shine and excel in every season.
Your purpose so clear . . . .
To let the world know that I am always near.
To lead and guide all that will ask,
No matter what . . . or how large the task.

I created you with a plan in mind . . .
And the scar you bear is my sign.
That you will every MOUNTAIN exceedingly climb!!

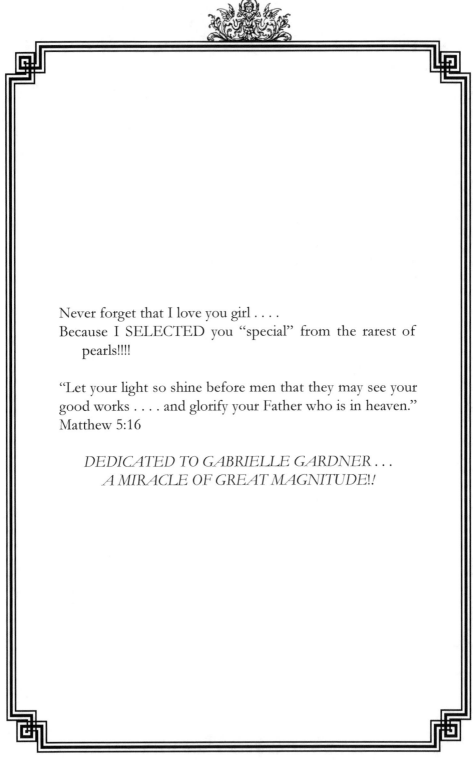

Never forget that I love you girl . . . .
Because I SELECTED you "special" from the rarest of
  pearls!!!!

"Let your light so shine before men that they may see your
good works . . . . and glorify your Father who is in heaven."
Matthew 5:16

DEDICATED TO GABRIELLE GARDNER . . .
A MIRACLE OF GREAT MAGNITUDE!!

AN ODE TO A—
GROUP OF THE LEAST
OF THESE

Their signs were held Ever so High . . . .
"WILL WORK FOR FOOD" . . . they read expecting a
    reply!
Focusing on one man . . . I shook my head in dread . . .
I had no food for him nor them.

But, the coins in my ash tray . . .
Reflecting the sunlight of the noon-day
Bid me to give it all plus more . . . .
Suddenly, recalling that my dear brother passed this way
    before . . .

And some good samaritan helped him when I couldn't
The distance between us or his whereabouts just
    wouldn't . . . .
Allow me to assist in his plight . . . .
An occasional call from him would often end in a fight.

I tried my very best . . . .
My searching never to manifest!
And as I approached the group of them and stopped.
I put all that I had in that man's pot . . . .

"Share please", I whispered looking in his sad eyes and
    weathered face.

How, I wondered did he get to this place.

Don't stare . . . but understand I declare . . . .

Except by the grace of God go I, and those that chose either to give or not to give this day . . .

We are all maybe just two paychecks away!!

I waved to the 'lot' of them as I slowly moved on . . . .

God bless you All . . . . Please know that He is still on the throne.

Car horns fervently blew . . . I said God bless you too, BECAUSE, one day it could be you!!

Matthew 25:40 . . . . *"Assuredly, I say to you inasmuch as you did it to the least of these My brethren, you did it to Me. "*

~~DEDICATED TO THE MEMORY OF MY BROTHER, SOLOMON MINOR~~

AND ABOVE ALL . . .
PERSEVERE

Oftentimes life's journey is riddled with pain . . .
Sometimes accompanied with torrential rain.
Yet we know that we must continue on . . .
One step at a time . . . before hope is gone.

We cannot give in, nor give up . . . No way . . .
So we face challenge after challenge anyway, any day.
Perseverance and endurance are tools for the fight . . .
When our struggles go far beyond the normal flight . . . .
But . . . we know by faith that joy will come with the
    morning light.

Even though steep hills still lurk before us . . .
It is in our Lord God we must totally trust.
What if we stopped in the middle of a storm unable to go
    on?
Questioning the words that faith is built upon . . . .
Questioning the promises that God gave His word on.

"I must go on, I cannot stop" . . . we say now . . . .
The bible, my roadmap has shown me how!!"
And so on we go, though the winds still blow; the trees
    sway.
We are reminded that the "stone" <u>was</u> rolled away . . .
On that third Day . . . they say.
For us and ours long ago . . .
That we might be careful not to extend our woe.

These trials come to make us stronger . . .
Although sometimes the tests seem longer!
Meanwhile . . . we pray without ceasing . . .
We praise God, being thankful for the pain now easing.

His grace is sufficient for these moments
Of Satan's underhanded torments.
Trying his best to undermine God's pledge . . .
And Keep us confused and on the edge.

This too shall pass . . . as we encounter one trial after another.
All too clear . . . we hear a whisper that sounds like mother.
"You can't stop now . . . life isn't going to always be easy . . .
Just remember to take His Yoke . . . . That's what IS easy."

And above all . . . . Persevere . . . .
And you will after the storm . . . . CHEER!!!!

"Come unto me all ye that labour and are heavy laden, and
I shall give you rest."
     "Take my yoke upon you and learn of me, for I am meek
and lowly in heart; and ye shall find rest unto your souls."
"For my yoke is easy, and my burden is light" Matthew
12:28-30,
     Dedicated to Tonia Yvette Minor—Benniefield

BABY BOOMER DIVAS
(60 PLUS!!)

"Diva 60" is the password she uses . . . .
"Di . . . Va" EXCLAIMS those that view us . . . and
  sometimes confuses us!!
But the mirrors do not lie we say . . .
As we continue to strut and sway . . .
Not unlike we did back in the day!!

Gravity has not been unkind to most . . .
FOR some however, it has been an ungracious host!
But let me focus just for a moment on my friends and
  me . . .
Some in stilettos even now you see!

Some of us wash the gray completely OUT . . .
While others keep the gray in and Shout . . .
"Hey check me out . . . .
Here I come with my short Do or natural curl . . .
Wig . . . Or something nice from "weave world"

"Oh my!!", the guys whistle . . . some younger, some older . . .
Guess my age? Our eyes wink . . . my have we gotten bolder!!
No crows feet giving our secret away . . . do we dare a fling . . .
We smile seductively, knowing our contacts are hiding the
  cholesterol ring!

Off to the gym we go . . .
Exercises moderate to slow . . . .
As we watch the younger ladies put on a show.
We don't hate though . . . .
Been there a while ago!!! . . .

Just trying to stay in shape . . .
while keeping a shape . . . .
Not the figure eight we once had
But a fuller one that's not half bad!

"Time to go now", we all chime . . .
Home for a shower and maybe some wine!!
My girls and I are oh so blessed . . .
Our health remains good test after test!!

We are on meds though, for one thing or another . . .
Realizing that we have become our mothers.
But everyday we thank our Master . . .
For one more Day without a disaster . . .

The bible reminds us of 3 score and ten . . .
We have reached 3 score, but only God knows our end!!

In the meantime . . . the Diva banner we will proudly wear . . .
Until the gentlemen no longer as much stare . . .
But in our minds we will Always be DIVAS . . .
And that My Sisters will Never Leave us!!

DEDICATED TO ALL of MY DIVA BUDDIES!!!

BLESSED ASSURANCES

The adversary yet again raised his head . . .
To a place that once to her was DREAD.
He tried to in her heart evoke fear again . . .
She stood steadfast though, for she knew that he would not
    win!!.

That old devil . . . . still up to his tricks and schemes . . .
He really ought be tired of losing it seems!!
You see, everyday she is fully armed . . .
For any and all battles . . . . God has clearly Warned . . .

These battles Are NOT yours, They are each one Mine.
Just continue to Trust in Me as you do all the time.
My assurances you have found are just five of many . . .
Fear not . . . I am your God . . . Are there others any?

Fear not, nor dismayed ye be . . .
For these blessed assurances are directly from Me . . .
You will be strengthened and upheld you see . . .
And your help coming from Me is for an eternity!!
My Joy and Peace I give to You . . .
When by Faith you declare this indeed is True!
Victory over the enemy she already has and smiles . . . .
Jesus is Mine, she says and has been all the while!

I am now commissioned to tell the world Of . . . .
My Savior, His promises And His Love.
Blessed assurances are the signs that to me appear . . .
And nothing, nor anyone shall ever I Fear!!
God then touched her . . . "For this new challenge, already
I am HERE . . . .
FEAR NOT, HE SAYS— . . . . I AM YOUR GOD, MY
DEAR!!"

DEDICATED TO A CANCER SURVIVOR, MY
FRIEND . . . .
JANIE BAKER BRUEN

"Fear not; for I am with thee: be not dismayed; for I am thy God: I
will strengthen thee; yea I will help thee; yea, I will uphold thee with
thy right Hand of my righteousness . . . Isaiah 41;10

CLOSER THAN
A SISTER?

A true and dear friend, in you have I truly found . . .
You are very unusual and quite profound.
Your uniqueness lies in the charm you possess . . .
And the love you show is just an attest . . .
Of Jesus in your heart no less!!

A rare gem whose value never decreases over time . . .
On the contrary, it increases as the hills of life's journey we
    climb.
Generous to a fault . . . her last she has given . . .
The cares of the" least of these" is how she is driven.

Her kindness is sprinkled with humorous antics . . .
The laughter she brings to our souls is not merely mechanic.
It's medicinal and so very soothing in times when it's
    needed . . .
I thank God daily for my benefits, which includes my friend
    indeed!!

Very confident and sassy . . . flirtatious, she is a diva . . . .
Watch out mister . . . she'll give you the blues and the
    "feva"!
Just beautiful inside and out . . . .
A treasure of assorted goodies no doubt.
A melodious voice as harmonious as a lark . . . .
Lifting the heads of the downtrodden out of places—dark.

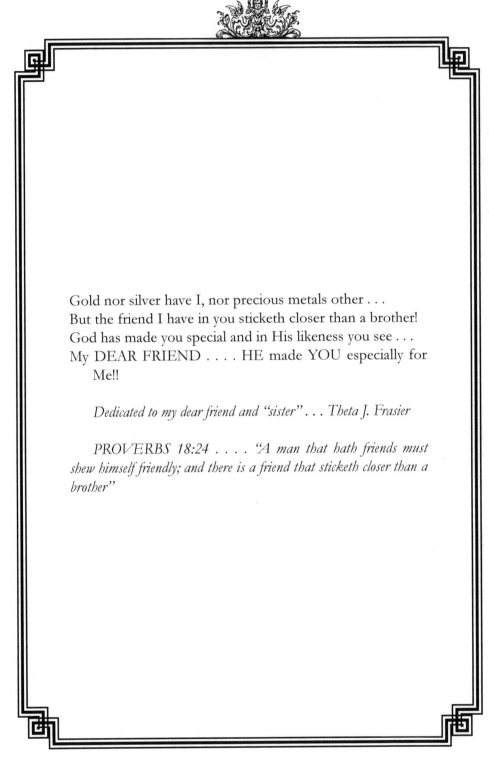

Gold nor silver have I, nor precious metals other . . .
But the friend I have in you sticketh closer than a brother!
God has made you special and in His likeness you see . . .
My DEAR FRIEND . . . . HE made YOU especially for
    Me!!

Dedicated to my dear friend and "sister" . . . Theta J. Frasier

PROVERBS 18:24 . . . . "A man that hath friends must shew himself friendly; and there is a friend that sticketh closer than a brother"

FAMILY BONDS

As she stood cutting her vegetables at the kitchen sink . . .
The tears she had held back were on the brink . . .
Of falling down her cheeks . . .
For she had been very hurt this week!!
By a family member she had been quite gracious to . . .
Why cry, she said when I know what to do . . . this is not new.

Just pray, family is here to stay . . . anyway.
All bonded with each others blood and genes
With love as the foundation, sewn at the seams!

As she proceeded to make her infamous Gumbo . . .
Her thoughts were now focused on who would show . . .
Dinner is at six . . . there is still a lot to fix!
She was preparing for at least twenty . . .
And if more than that, there would be plenty!

They came in droves . . . more than had been anticipated . . .
All were received . . . the older ones first while the young
    waited.
They entered and all appeared in great character . . .
Greeting each other with hugs and laughter!
Then they gathered in the den for the prayer and blessing . . .
The matriarch of the family stood after assessing.
"Hold hands and form that circle that can't be broken", she
    requested . . .
Everyone complied to what she had suggested.

Dear heavenly Father, she began . . . we honor you today . . .
For the many blessings you have sent our way . . . .
And as she continued the prayer the hostess looked up and
    was very pleased . . . .
This is my family . . . ! Love them no matter their deeds.

In spite of our flaws and faults . . . we realize our charge to
    keep
Exhorting, comforting, and caring . . . on each one we must
    heap!
Listening, helping, befriending . . . never offending!
Careful of advising . . . that's a tough call . . .
Sometimes it's taken for judging after all!!

We cannot our families select . . . .
Which is why God and Love are the bonds that connect!!

After the prayer, they embraced one after the other . . .
God admonishes that we love one another . . . .
And to every Family member no matter the problem . . .
If we can't . . . God can solve them . . .
To Him in prayer we take all of our cares and concerns . . .
He has the answers to them all . . . we must learn!

The hostess went to the one that she had been hurt by . . .
To her surprise, he started to cry . . .
And said I am so sorry . . . forgive me please . . .
She gave him a kiss to put his mind at ease!!
Not to worry . . . I still love you she said
He replied simply . . . I love you too and he smiled as he
    raised his head,
That was all that was needed . . .
Come all . . . let us now eat . . . she pleaded!!

Around the table they sat ready for the meal . . . .
Enamored with the fellowship that sealed the family deal!!

ENOUGH said . . . .
Pass the Gumbo, a little child said
Then another . . . . Is there any corn bread?????
She smiled . . . . Families hmm . . . you gotta love 'em!!!

*DEDICATED TO FAMILIES EVERYWHERE . . . BUT
ESPECIALLY MINE!!*

FOR EXCELLENCE . . .
STRIVE

Mediocrity . . . . somewhere in the middle of nowhere . . . .

Among words synonymous to average, adequate, acceptable, . . . don't go there!!

With posters on the walls of classrooms . . . teachers declare . . .

"Mediocrity is not an option"_ in here or anywhere!

And if you are there . . . move up to the next stage . . . .

Excellence is what you are striving for . . . so engage!!

Amid the distractions . . . .

Amid the difficulty of fractions . . . .

Amid peer pressure . . .

Amid environmental stressors . . . .

Amid the decadence of morality . . . .

Amid the disrespect . . . almost now in totality!!

Go right now to the head of the class . . .

And not a question should be asked.

Find the eagles and like them soar . . . .
Leave those chickens on the barnyard floor!
Yes, leave them right where they are . . . they won't go far . . .
They have no desire to become a star!

Now, know . . . Hard work and diligence imminently await . . . .
Honor roll or perhaps a Nobel prize could be your fate!

Yet . . . know that excellence not only applies to the classroom . . .
But . . . in any and all endeavors . . . . excellence is our heirloom!
It is after all our birthright . . . .
We <u>are</u> made in God's image . . . is that not right?
The songwriter exclaims "Oh How Excellent is His name in all the Earth!!"
Therefore for excellence you <u>must</u> strive . . . AND YOU <u>WILL</u> find IT'S WORTH!!

DEDICATED TO STUDENTS EVERYWHERE . . .
ESPECIALLY MINE (FORMER AND PRESENT)
AND THE YOUTH AT BETHLEHEM MISSIONARY
BAPTIST CHURCH!

GRANDMA'S TOUCH

A grandmother's touch . . . really means so much . . . .
Her warm hands and cuddly arms, I gladly clutch!
She brings joy to the very core of my heart . . .
Her antics and sayings . . . and that voice like a lark.

I share all of me and want to . . . 'cause she so nice . . .
And in all matters of the heart . . . I await her advice.
She has lots of wisdom to give . . . .
Lots of love, too . . . . without it, I just couldn't live!!

She spoils me rotten . . .
Helps me out when, in trouble I've gotten!!
She sees the best in me and tells me so . . .
I am her cup of "tea" . . . . she says so!

Not a day will pass without a kind word spoken . . .
Or gifts of love . . . or some small token . . .

Thank you grandma . . . I love you so much . . .
For all you do and most especially, your majestic touch!!

HAVE FUN . . . . DANCE

Dancing, dancing, dancing . . . feet just moving . . .
Swaying to the music . . . . stepping and grooving.
Swinging to the beat . . . onlookers out of their seats.
Cheering and applauding . . . . stomping and clapping.
Oh what a night . . . my shirttail flapping.

Carefree and happy . . . Just having fun . . .
No worries or issues just plain old fun!
This gift was passed down from Mom and Dad . . .
As kinfolk told of the great time they had had!
Money was thrown at Dad's feet . . . they say
While Mom collected . . . how sweet the pay!

I often think of them . . . . when I dance . . .
And enjoy every minute as I prance.
"Cut the rug!" . . . the crowd began to shout . . . .
As I twirled with hands high turning about.
Hips moving with a thrust that was legit . . .
Gyrating was not included . . . not one bit!

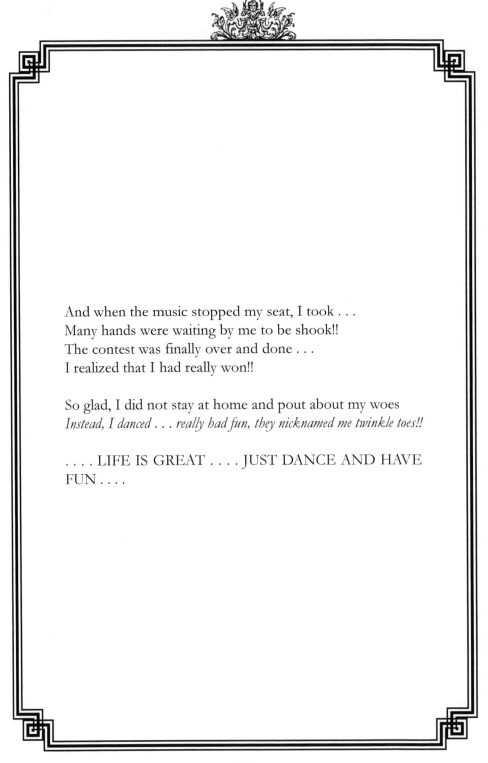

And when the music stopped my seat, I took . . .
Many hands were waiting by me to be shook!!
The contest was finally over and done . . .
I realized that I had really won!!

So glad, I did not stay at home and pout about my woes
Instead, I danced . . . really had fun, they nicknamed me twinkle toes!!

. . . . LIFE IS GREAT . . . . JUST DANCE AND HAVE
FUN . . . .

IN ADORATION OF
MOTHER

Mother dear, I adore you . . . .
For there is nobody really quite like you!
The love you have given to me . . . .
Is unequivocally a gift from God, you see . . .

An abundance of virtues you came equipped with . . .
To give to us the same . . . God knew you would do it.
Our journey as yours would be long . . .
And in your heart, He gave you songs!

To sing when heartaches came . . .
To sing when they called us names!
To sing when we were persecuted . . .
To sing when we were disrespected!

You placed our heads in your bosom close . . .
And soothed and comforted near your heart of course . . .
Thank you mother for shaping my character . . .
Thank you mother for making me kinder . . .

For molding my integrity . . .
For teaching morality . . .
For giving me a system of values . . .
For showing me the importance of valor.
For allowing God to come into my heart . . .
And now that I know Him . . . we will never part.

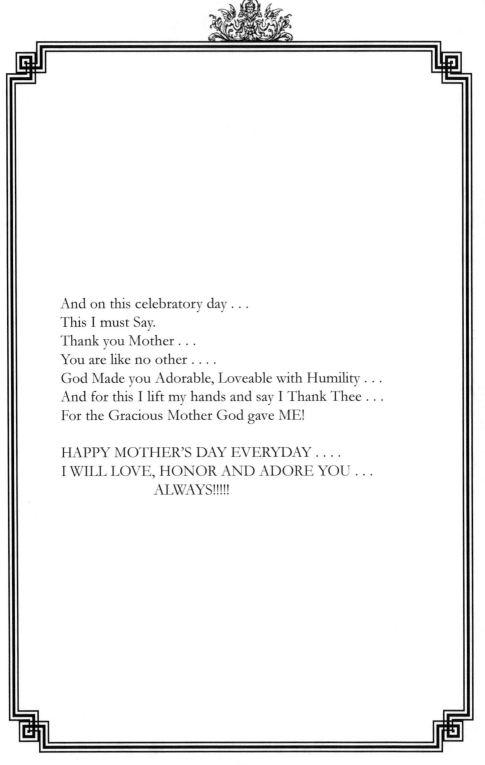

And on this celebratory day . . .
This I must Say.
Thank you Mother . . .
You are like no other . . . .
God Made you Adorable, Loveable with Humility . . .
And for this I lift my hands and say I Thank Thee . . .
For the Gracious Mother God gave ME!

HAPPY MOTHER'S DAY EVERYDAY . . . .
I WILL LOVE, HONOR AND ADORE YOU . . .
ALWAYS!!!!!

KINDRED SPIRITS

A beautiful lady walked into the room one day . . .
"Good morning all", she said, as we looked her way.
We bid her the same greeting . . .

Then suddenly we were summoned to the morning meeting.
The lady and I sat at the same table . . . we both were new . . .

But the words between us were few.
There was an air of aristocracy about her . . . .

No doubt a caliber above others!
Could it be she felt a sense of superiority??

But then she smiled at me, and the warmth of it touched me . . .
Her inner spirit was revealed suddenly.
There was something in her spirit that leapt to mine . . .

Noticeably a connection of some kind . . .
As days passed we began to share commonalities . . .

We found we both had similar personalities!!!
On rare occasions tears were shed . . . .

Realizing on some issues our hearts had bled . . .
The two of us had put on paper our innermost thoughts . . .

And both had released some battles we had fought.
Who would have guessed that day we met . . .

That we would share through poetry things we could not
   forget.
The fondness grew as we continued to share . . . .
Judging people by their outer appearances . . . beware!!
God places strangers in our midst for special reasons . . .

HE calls them angels and they appear in and out of season.
Thank you God for my angel, I pray . . .

And I wish in my life she would certainly stay!!!!
But if per chance that cannot be . . .
I shall e're remember the "kindred spirits" . . . she and me!!

Dedicated to Z. Watts

JOY FOR MOTHERS

A mother's joy is felt most when she is proud . . .
Of her children's success way above the clouds!
The journey there, took more effort than you know . . .
Notwithstanding opposing foes!!

Patience, endurance and God's grace . . .
Were there when such obstacles were faced.
Mother taught all that was needed, though . . .
Virtues of integrity, goodness, and character, I know!

Perseverance, endurance nor values were neglected . . .
Mother knew that these would keep you erected . . .
When the chips fell as expected!!

And now that it's all said and done . . .
Mother is now smiling broadly . . . pointing at her daughter
    or son!
When a competition of sorts they had won!
She is bursting with pride and joy . . . her heart filled with
    love . . . .
Rewards of her labor . . . She praises her Lord above

Bless you Lord, my child has reached yet another goal.
Please continue to Bless my children as they strive to
    uphold . . .
Their rightful place in society's mold!

LAUGHTER,
THE GREAT . . . REMEDY

The joke for the day was eagerly anticipated . . .
What a day it had been, a hearty laugh would be appreciated!
A day of gloom and doom . . . . relief was needed and
     SOON!!

There he is they pointed . . . .
In just a few minutes we will all be disjointed!!
"The doctor is here now" . . . . he imparted . . .
We started laughing before the joke even started!!

His delivery was filled with expectancy . . .
One had already fallen to her knees . . .
Another . . . oh stop it please . . .
Yet wringing her hands in total glee!!
One jumped three feet off the floor . . .
Begging . . . no more . . . can't take no more.

And when the joke was completed and we were again composed . . .
Tissue was given as we blew our noses . . .
Tears were streaming down our faces . . .
And work was now one of the happiest places!!

Once again, Joe had given us his remedy for life's difficulties . . .
"In these present conditions", he said . . . take heed . . . .
Laughter is really the medicine we all need!

Bartlett Middle School . . . '80s

Dedicated to my friends, Joseph, Betty, Eldora, my girls, and most of all my mother Gladys P. They made my spirit lighter…they made me laugh!!

PLEASE . . . A LITTLE LUCK

Ching-a-ling . . . three cherries on the reel, ring . . .
Only two double diamonds on the next one sling . . .
And she's not winning a doggone thing!!

"Come on", she thought . . . slots were once kind . . .
And the pay-offs were all too fine!!
She was called the "Queen of the Slots "
That Lady's luck was envied by many . . . she was hot!!

And now . . . she spins . . . and never wins . . . .
Must she call it quits then?!!
Never!! . . . she said as she shook her head!

Luck is merely happenstance . . . .
Remember . . . it's not guaranteed . . . . it's only a chance!!
Here today, gone tomorrow, back the next day . . .
So the lady whispers to the old slot machine . . .
With much confidence as she leans . . .
And talking to it with ease . . .
She asks . . . Can I have my luck back? Please!
And with anticipation and expectancy . . .
She spins that reel and waits patiently . . .
For that bell to ring . . .
JACKPOT WINNER . . . they all again sing!!!

That lady's luck is now back!!! The "little luck" she
    requested is now a Fact.
PERHAPS I WILL TRY HER ANTIC . . . .
IT CAN'T HURT . . . CAN IT!!

PRETTY LITTLE
DARK-SKINNED GIRL

"Hey there "pretty little dark-skinned girl . . . .
Skin so dark and smooth, enhancing teeth like pearls.
Blessed with the pigment eu-mela-nin in abundance . . .
Protecting your skin from the sun rays nuisance!

Sweetie, you won't age for years to come . . . .
Give credence to the descendants you have hailed from!
Celebrate your rich chocolate hue . . . .
Don't let another send you askew!!

With remarks unmerited and unkind . . . .
Which places you unfortunately in a wretched state of
    mind!!
Anger has no grounds . . . . no not one in this world.
Smile instead, you are the majestic one, girl

Celebrate the elegance of the dark skinned queens . . . .
From the motherland of Africa . . . . and their high
    self-esteem!
Celebrate your heritage with joy and gladness . . .
Let the mirror that you peek into reflect
your happiness!!

Celebrate the richness of that beautiful hue . . . .
Having been endowed with it . . . girl this really becomes
    you!!
The word on the street is that "black don't crack" . . . (shhh)
The truth of the matter is . . . that's really a fact!
Celebrate and be sassy with the skin you are in . . . .
Your rich darkness is really a win-win!!
And Now hear this . . . .
WITH your HEAD HELD HIGH, STANDING TALL . . .
"Pretty little dark-skinned girl." . . . .
YOU are really "THE FAIREST OF ALL"!!

> _Dedicated to dark-skinned_
> _Girls everywhere!!!!_

OH DEAR FRIEND OF MINE

Oh dear friend of mine . . . .
You have always been so kind . . . .
Even when I whimper and whine!
You Let me do this . . . if I need to
It's your compassion and love . . . thank you!

Complaining even of my woes . . .
You tell me of the thorns on a rose.
Thank you, my friend for the parable you chose.
Find the beauty . . . no matter the situation, you say . . . .
Things will get better . . . they do anyway!!

My friend, you are a bible scholar far above many . . .
Your direction to a verse often calmed my anxiety.
Your listening ear is always there for my heartaches and
    pain.
You speak volumes of wisdom from God . . . which has
    often helped me to sustain.

You have defended me whether right or wrong . . .
Because your love for me is that strong!!

Probably had to "cuss" a tad bit, though . . .
But refused to let it show.
It went unchallenged every time . . . .
You took that position for me, that was a sign . . .
Of a true friend . . .
Until the immortal end!!!
You have always let me be just who I am . . .
Never judgmental . . . you took that stand!

Sometimes we talk for hours at a time . . .
Sharing secrets for a lifetime!
Laughing heartily at anecdotes or some absurd antic.
At times we were hysterical and frantic.
That's when it's real funny . . . O-M-G!!!

I will hold our friendship so dear . . .
And of losing it, I will never fear!!

And please know this dear friend of mine . . . .
Our "Friend Ship" sails just FINE!!

And My Love for you will NEVER END . . . My Dear
   Friend!!

Dedicated to Ruby Rawlison and Betty Keitt

THE RAINBOW'S END

Somewhere there is an end to the rainbow . . .
And a pot of gold awaits you, I'm told.
On several occasions I tried to reach it . . .
The journey was long . . . I grew tired of it!
Instead, I now just look forward to seeing it in the sky . . .
After the storms have passed by.
And the myth is just that!!! . . . Oh drat!!.

After the storms are over in your life . . .
And you have endured struggles and strife . . .
Look forward to the beautiful rainbow that will appear . . .
With it's band of colors so vibrant and clear.
The sign so clear . . . God's Promise so dear . . .
The Rainbow, God said is My promise so true . . .
It has no end . . . and it's fortune is my Love for you!

RESTING IN HIS CARE

Under the Wings of His Care,
Is Janice P. Duncan so fair, so rare;
A woman that has stood the test
And is STILL standing in His rest.

For God knew that she would remember,
His promise never to leave her,
Nor forsake, nor abandon her.

God is the giver and keeper of life . . .
Amid all of 'its battles and strife.
God knew, Janice, that you knew, that nothing is impossible
And by faith, YOU know that all things Are Possible.

God knew that you would be an inspiration to all of us,
And we looked as you . . . to God in Trust.
Yes, Janice He knew that he could count on you, to tell of
    His Amazing Grace . . .
TO His children who too, are trying to run Life's RACE!
SO . . . Hold on my sister . . . Cheer up!!
And Continue to Look up . . .
God is Looking DOWN . . . Spreading Blessings Abound!!

Psalm 121:1-2 "I will lift mine eyes to the hills—From whence cometh my help . . . . My help comes from the Lord, Who made heaven and earth."
DEDICATED TO JANICE DUNCAN
And now in memory of a Great warrior having battled her illness for 27 years . . . Now rest in His peace!!

RETIREMENT . . .
NOW WHAT

Now that you are retired . . . what do you do?
Nothing . . . . OR any doggone thing YOU want to do!!
A fulfilling career is over and done . . .
A new phase of life has just begun!

Now what really is next you ask . . . .
Let it be whatever you like . . . don't make it a task!!

If you want to . . . . Sleep all day . . . .
In those PJ's you can't throw away . . . .
Go fishing if you wish . . . it's your call . . . .
Shop till you drop, just don't fall . . .
Don't need anything broken . . . there are so many malls!
Have a glass of wine at noon-day . . . .
You are not working . . . it's okay . . .
Clean the house from bottom to top . . .
Plant that long overdue garden . . . then on the sofa flop . . .
Watch TV all day long . . .
Answer your emails . . . it's been so long!
Babysit the grands . . . but know it's your option . . .
And remind YOUR kids that it's not an adoption.
Take a cruise with your significant other or someone . . .
Eat, drink and just have plenty of fun . . .
You deserve all that's good under the Sun.

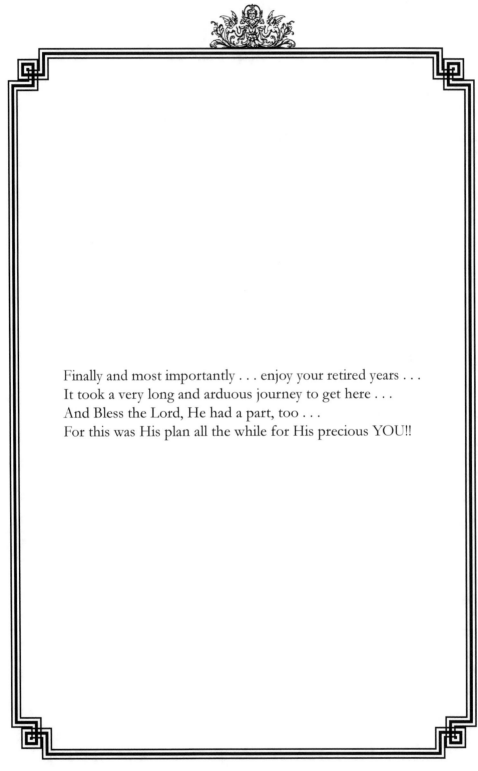

Finally and most importantly . . . enjoy your retired years . . .
It took a very long and arduous journey to get here . . .
And Bless the Lord, He had a part, too . . .
For this was His plan all the while for His precious YOU!!

RUBIES, DIAMONDS
AND PEARLS

Precious gems so valued and rare . . .
Treasures found in nature's care!
My friends are as valuable and as dear . . . .
My precious jewels I call them, and bless the Lord that they
　　are here.

Rubies brilliantly glowing in shades of red . . .
Celebrated by bible scholars "as the gem of gems", it's been
　　said.
A firm friendship as been associated with it, I'm told.
I have known a few steadfast friends that I dearly behold.

Diamonds shining ever so brightly . . .
From Carbon pressured and squeezed tightly!!
I have known friends with gripping hugs after my falls . . .
They picked me up . . . never ever leaving me to deal with
　　it all.
Always there with the skills for which they were equipped . . .
Volumes of wisdom and biblical quotes spew from their
　　lips.
Oftentimes, all that was needed was a lending ear . . . .
This gem like my special friends, I hold near and dear!!

And at last, the noted pearl . . .
From the oyster it came to our world!!
Cultured naturally in varying sizes, shapes and forms . . . .
Cherished as symbols of purity, perfection far above the norm!
Elegant and untarnished are descriptors more . . . .
My friends have the same characters . . . Whom I lovingly adore!

Grateful am I that my precious gems are my dearest friends . . .
Have been by my side time and time again.
On every occasion . . . good or bad . . . .
In happy moments and in those that were sad!!

What can I say except thank you so much . . .
Angels you are and will remain as such . . . .
God had a master plan and you were to be a part . . .
My precious gems . . . rubies, diamonds, and pearls . . . .
I love you with all of my heart!!

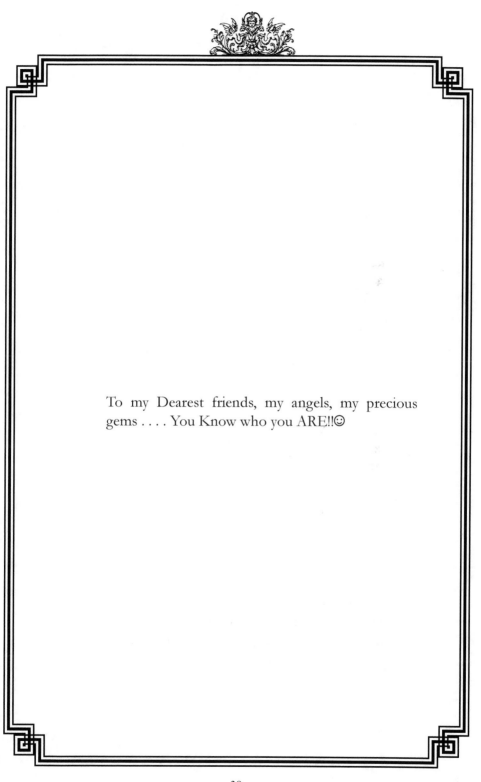

To my Dearest friends, my angels, my precious gems . . . . You Know who you ARE!!☺

SUMMERTIME A'INT
ALWAYS EASY

"Summertime and the living is easy" . . . from Porgy and
    Bess . . .
Mama crooned happily and I swayed nonetheless.
As far back as I can remember that song my favorite.
Sang for me by many . . . and on instruments others played
    it!

It symbolized life at it's fullest and best, with all of it's
    frills . . .
Sunshine, blue skies, blueberries on the hills!
Each summer I looked forward to . . . swimming, camping
    and playing . . .
Going to Grannie's house, where I so enjoyed staying!!
Why in that song were no lyrics about the Storms, I now
    ask?
Having weathered a few . . . no one knew . . . I wore well a
    mask.

Hidden from view to most were tears that flowed . . .
Only to my mother and grandmother, I showed!
"Hush little baby don't you cry" . . . the lyrics bellowed . . .
But I cried nevertheless . . . as storm after storm followed!
With their winds raging and thunder roaring . . .
Blindsided by the lightning, while the rain was pouring.

No mention of storms was ever in that song . . . .
That I had loved for so long!!

But Alas . . . "Your Daddy is rich" . . . . My heavenly Father
    that is!!
In houses and land, with cattle on a thousand hills . . .
My life in His hands, and it is still His will!!

He won't put anymore on you than you can bear . . .
Sometimes though, it really doesn't seem fair.
Then there above the horizon . . . a rainbow I see . . .
And clouds with silver linings all beckoning me.
Above the thunder, I remember hearing this . . . .
The "Plans" for you my child do still exist!!

He holds my hand and says" Now hush My little baby, don't
    you cry" . . .
For You and yours, I did die!!!!!
That YOU would have life ABUNDANTLY.
"My" promise I keep most Definitely!!

YES "Summer Time ". . . I now sing to my daughter . . .
I just ought to, and she will sing to hers . . .
And down through the years it will be sung to others.
It is still a song that I will always love.

As I go though the storms of life with Him who is in
    heaven above.
"Trust Me in all things", God admonishes and you will
    see . . .
That "Summer Time Is Easy" indeed in ME!

"For I know that the plans I have for you, said the Lord,
    thoughts of peace and not evil, to give you an expected
    end". Jeremiah 29:11

DEDICATED TO MY DAUGHTER:
Ronetta Arvitrius Milner—Gardner

THE BEAUTIFUL GIFT

Oh what a beautiful baby boy . . . .
Born of a virgin to bring the world abundant joy!
Soon to be King of the universe . . .
God sent His Son and He is First!

Alpha and Omega, the beginning and the ending.
He came to save an earth from sin impending.
It is no secret that the world awaited His Presence . . .
The epitome of Perfection, the essence of Excellence!!

He lay in a lowly manger . . . .
Where the cattle and sheep were no strangers!
The shepherds and wise men all came that night . . . .
Following a spectacular star . . . to an amazing sight.

The wise men brought gifts of fortunes untold . . .
Nothing too good for the Messiah, the scriptures foretold!
The angels jubilantly sang "hallelujah" in the heavenly
    choir . . .
Melodiously harmonizing, and magnificently attired!!

The babe's earthly mother and father were in awe of this
    gift . . .
That had come to give the world a most desired lift!
Mary and Joseph were chosen by God Himself . . .
God had seen their humility and would trust no one else!
This gift was far too precious to be in another's hand . . .
For this gift from God would save the Land . . .

He would bring hope to those in despair . . .
Hearts that were broken would be repaired . . .
The lost would be found and freed . . .
The blind in spirit would find vision indeed . . .

Peace and happiness in Him would be found . . .
Shackles would be removed from those that were bound . . .
Joy unspeakable would be in the hearts of many . . . .
And by faith, burdens would not be any!!
"Come Let Us Adore" this beautiful gift that has been
    given"
To all that believe in Him sent to us from heaven!
How Marvelous; How Wonderful; How Amazing . . . is this
    Beautiful Gift . . . .
And to God be the Glory and in Praise our hands we lift.
                    THANK YOU GOD!!

A TEACHER'S HEART

A teacher's heart is filled with love . . . .
Given immeasurably from the master above.
For this profession, God chose only the best . . .
He only called those, whose hearts could stand the test.

It took, he knew . . . a special heart . . .
That could love all children, and call them all smart.
The task would not be easy, by any means to educate.
So He selected those that would be dedicated . . . .

To a profession not nearly as revered as it should be.
Yet, they would continue their mission EXTRAORDINARILY!!
Their passion would be clearly recognized . . . .
As they taught child after child . . . that was their prize!!

Now Let us take a moment to reflect . . .
Monuments of teachers we should erect . . .
In a park in every town . . . .
Hands down!!!
All that had a teacher should not only honor them . . .
But respect, regard and love them!

For their patience and the ways they encourage . . . .
For their wisdom, understanding and knowledge . . .
For their genuine concern each day . . . .
(every year usually from August to May) . . . .
For their kindness and their wit . . . .
(In classes of thirty or more they really needed it)

For their hearts of gold . . .
For the mysteries they unfold . . . .
For the many hats they have worn . . .
For the way they've handled ridicule and scorn . . .
Bless a teacher with the praise they deserve . . .
Becoming a teacher takes a lot of nerve!!

The pay should be far above scale . . .
But the rewards for their labor do prevail!
When the "light bulb" comes on in a small child's Head . . .
"I got it teacher" . . . just like you said!!!

The joy in their hearts overflows . . . .
And their love for this job shows . . . .
and everybody knows!!
Hats off to them that are called by God's intervention.
And are obedient to that calling for it may not have been
     their first intention.
You know I heard a student once proclaim . . . .
If not for a teacher, could I even spell my NAME???

This poem is dedicated to all teachers in my profession!
All that have a heart to love and teach children . . . ,
     even the ones that _appear_ to be unteachable and even
     unloveable!!!

Lynda Minor Milner, retired teacher ☺!

THE MITOSIS SAGA
(MITOSIS . . . REALLY . . .
REALLY NEEDED)

Mitosis is a continuous process we can't live without!
Necessary for growth, development and healing, no doubt.
It can be observed in stages of four . . . .
With Cytokinesis and Interphase after and before.

PMAT is the acronym that helps us remember . . . .
Prophase, Metaphase, Anaphase and Telephase are it's members.
In stage one, the nuclear membrane breaks down . . . .
Centrosomes with centrioles move around . . . .
Then they stop at the opposite poles . . . .
With the spindles attached . . . a very important role . . .
In stage two the chromosomes line up at the equator . . .
In stage three, the chromatids are pulled at the poles after . . .
And in the last stage, which completes the process . . .
Two identical somatic cells are the results . . . no more, no less!!
This was an activity on cells from Biology 101 . . . *(Mary Knight's 9ᵗʰ grade class 2013)*
So you see Science can be FUN!!!!!!

THE TAPESTRY OF LIFE

As the old woman gazed upon her patchwork quilt . . .
Interwoven patches of wool, cotton polyester, ... even
    silk . . .
Threaded together sequentially . . . . one patch after another
Each row arranged orderly one beneath the other!

Much to her amazement this was symbolic of the cycle of
    life no doubt . . .
An array of colors and patterns arranged in an exquisite
    tapestry inside and out!
"This looks like a reflection of my life . . . and its many
    facets" . . . .
With it's liabilities . . . . but more importantly . . . it's assets!!

She couldn't help but smile . . . . She had no regrets . . . .
She looked at the first patch representing . . . life's Alpha/
    Beginning . . .
. . . . the last it's Omega/ ending . . . .
The first Row reflective of life's early stages . . . "When I
    was child", I spake as one . . .
Each subsequent row indicative of life's remaining flow . . .
It had been a long and arduous journey . . . of up-hills and
    valleys low . . . .
Relationships, family, a livelihood, celebrations . . . moments
    of joy and moments of woe!
The sum total of life in an order ordained by God
    Himself . . .

"I know the plans I have for you and no-one else!"
She then looked at the last patch, which mirrored her life's
   end . . . .
It was near . . . her time had come . . . The last stitch . . . .
   the setting of her sun!
Now in retrospect, had she fulfilled the purpose that from
   God had come?
Did she love her neighbors and treat her fellowman
   right!! . . .

Had she loved her family when things weren't always bright!
Did she feed the hungry and the poor—sustain . . .
Encourage the sick and those in pain.

Had she lifted the spirits of the downtrodden . . . .
Reassuring they would never be forgotten!
Had she assembled with saints for prayer and worship.
Had she read the bible, heard sermons and been diligent in
   stewardship!
Yes. she said weakly, but with conviction . . . her words
   slightly faltered . . . .
I did Lord just as my steps by you were ordered . . . .
Just then she heard Gabriel's Horn . . .
Her "time to die" as a result of her "time to be born"!
And as the last stitch in the last patch had been pinned . . .
Her last glance reflected the tapestry's end . . . time for her
   stopped then!
God was pleased as he took her hand . . . "Well done" He
   said . . . . come on in!!

THIS DAY, I . . .

This day I, will lift mine eyes to the heavens above . . .
    And thank my God for life and His love.
This day I, will cast on the Lord all of my cares . . . .
    And try to help Him . . . I would not dare!

This day I, will promise not to allow to pass . . . .
    Without achieving at least one important task!
This day I, will make someone smile . . . .
    And comfort one that may be in a trial.

This day I, will smell the flowers . . . .
    And read a book maybe for hours.
This day I will take a brisk walk . . . .
    And phone an old friend and talk.

This day I, will wink at the sun . . . .
    And follow the cloud-formations . . . just for fun!
This day I, will find some good in my fellowman . . .
    Regardless of the injustices and all that's wrong in this land.

This day I, will ultimately and wholly enjoy . . .
    And allow nothing or no one rob me of my joy.
This day I, will not waste on triviality nor frivolity . . .
    For you see, this day didn't really have to be.

This day was a gift indeed
Tomorrow may never proceed . . .
And so, now as I watch the sun set at the close of this day . . .
    I bless the Lord once more and only for this DAY!!!

WHISPERS OF LOVE

Weeping for me, I know, was a must . . .
And you leaned heavily on God, whom you will forever
    trust.
Tears streamed steadily . . . your heart was broken . . . .
Words at moments were even unspoken . . . .
The depth of the pain could not a measure yield . . .
Well-wishers were sympathetic . . . but, the agony they
    could not feel.

Time is the healer that will be effective . . . .
Yet . . . I am with you always . . . we are still connected.
Etched forever in your heart and memory bank
Along with items of memorabilia and even some
pranks.
Oh, by the way . . . I got my wings today . . . a perfect fit!!
They placed me in the group with the humor and wit.
Go figure . . . . I did make them laugh a bit!!

That made you smile . . . I know . . .
Now let me to places show . . .
You . . . where I can be found . . . .
And not at all will it astound!

You will find me in a song . . . . ,
Remember, the ones we sang along?
In the laughter of a <u>good</u> joke . . . .
Not the bad ones . . . at which we often poked.

I can be found sitting on a fluffy Cumulus cloud . . .

Legs and feet dangling . . . looking down at the crowd.

Found In the brightness of a sun-filled day . . .
Beckoning the rain clouds . . . to stay away!!
In the moon beams that light the night . . .
And among the stars that twinkle so bright.

In a gentle breeze, I'll whisper ever so sweetly . . .
Of the love that will last throughout eternity.
On the windows, I'll tap when the rain falls . . . .
But in your heart most of all . . .
There, forever I will remain . . .
Until lovingly, we embrace again!!

Joy will come . . . trust me my dear love . . .
AS I CONTINUE TO WHISPER To you FROM ABOVE!!!

"Weeping may endure for a night, but JOY cometh in the morning"
Psalms 30:5

Dedicated to Brenda Gardner and Family . . . .
    In memory of "Cam"